I0201917

Prayer That Saves
A Scriptural Guide to Intercession for the Lost

Cynthia Cadiente

Hawak Kamay Publishing
P.O. Box 933
Raeford, NC 28376
www.HawakKamayPublishing.com

Copyright © 2021 Cynthia Cadiente
All rights reserved.

Scripture quotations are from the ESV® Bible (The Holy Bible, English Standard Version®), copyright © 2001 by Crossway, a publishing ministry of Good News Publishers. Used by permission. All rights reserved.

ISBN: 978-1-7370988-1-2

CONTENTS

Introduction

As you crack the cover of this booklet, you may already have someone specific on your heart. You may have begun to pray for them, or perhaps for a group or a nation you feel called to minister to. You may have been praying for someone for years, with little fruit to show for it. You may be exhausted from a long, metaphorical night of prayer, or you may be falling to your knees in intercession for the first time. However this book finds you, my hope is that you will be encouraged and enlightened by its words.

The inspiration for this guide was my own salvation experience. Having been raised by a pastor and homeschooled by my mother, I thought I knew it all. There was nothing anyone could have told me to bring me to the cross, repentant, without the Holy Spirit's urging me first. It is my belief, based on what you will read in these chapters, that my family's intercession led to that urging and ultimately to my salvation.

While researching for this project, these biblical teachings took on new life for me as an intercessor, as well as a beneficiary of prayer. I began to see the unsaved people around me through different eyes. As I wrote each chapter, its completion was followed by encounters with the subject matter in my personal life. For that reason, I designed this short and concise booklet to easily slip into a Bible cover, so that it can serve as a quick reference and a handy reminder. Each of these lessons will arise more than once on your intercession journey, as I can attest to myself. Make notes in this book, highlight in it, dog-ear the pages that are most pertinent to you. Make use of the spaces provided to record your prayers, so you can look back over time and see how God's hand was always at work even when you were unaware.

The passages referenced in this book are just a taste of the examples found in scripture. I encourage you to dig a little deeper on your own, as other biblical examples may apply more specifically to your situation. This is meant to be a basic guide to intercessory prayer as taught in scripture, not a comprehensive theological study into the general subject of prayer.

As you embark on this journey to intercession for the lost, my own prayers go with you. This will not be an easy road. You will find no magic words, no formulas – only the promises God offers to those who will walk in His ways.

> *"But seek first the kingdom of God and his righteousness, and all these things will be added to you."*
>
> *Matthew 6:33*

A Cloud of Witnesses

"Therefore, since we are surrounded by so great a cloud of witnesses, let us also lay aside every weight, and sin which clings so closely, and let us run with endurance the race that is set before us, looking to Jesus, the founder and perfecter of our faith..."

Hebrews 12:1-2

I was fifteen years old, standing in a crowd with others worshiping Jesus together at the Assemblies of God General Council, when I had a vision. In my mind's eye, I was running, carrying a torch that had no flame. I was exhausted, covered in sweat. My hair was tied back, but strands of it got loose and stuck to my face. I was slowing down. The torch was too heavy, and it wasn't even lit. I wondered why I was running at all.

Voices, beginning as a whisper, surrounded me. The words overlapped, but I knew by the reverent tones that they were each speaking to God. The torch I was carrying ignited. Among the prayers, I recognized the voices of my grandparents – both living and passed. Then, this cloud of voices all increased in volume and in fervor, crying out to God on my behalf. I felt the flame within me grow as the torch blazed and my strength was renewed. I ran, and I was filled with a desire for one thing – to bring glory to the God who saved me.

It would be sixteen years before the meaning of that vision would come to light. I used to look for signs everywhere as I perfected my Christian act, and so I spent the years following this event searching for the interpretation. I thought I must be something special.

When I finally heard God's call to drop the act, repent and follow him, this vision made sense. It wasn't about me. It was about my spiritual ancestors – all the way back to Adam – who had interceded for the generations of lost lambs to come. Their prayers, constantly before the Father, were the key to my repentance and decision to follow Jesus.

In my testimony, which is published on my blog[1], I state that "no amount of preaching would have saved me." This is true. I had heard more preaching before I could read than most do in a lifetime. I believe that the day I felt the weight of my sins and turned from them was a direct result of my family's prayer for me.

> *"No one can come to me unless the Father who sent me draws him."*
>
> *John 6:44*

This does not negate evangelism. We are called to spread the gospel, each to our respective mission fields. (*Matthew 28:19-20*) However, the focus of this book is on intercessory prayer, specifically for the salvation of the lost. This is the side of evangelism that your loved one may never witness, as it will be conducted in private between you and Jesus.

In Hebrews, we are encouraged to run forward with perseverance. We are promised that while we do so we are benefiting from the prayers of those who have gone before. How incredible to think that Paul's prayers, sent up hundreds of years ago, would be brought before God on our behalf today!

---

[1] www.cynthiacadiente.com/post/thepiece

"… the four living creatures and the twenty-four elders fell down before the Lamb, each holding a harp, and golden bowls full of incense, which are the prayers of the saints."

Revelation 5:8

You, who have opened this book to learn how you can pray for a loved one's soul, are a voice within that great cloud of witnesses mentioned in Hebrews. Your prayers, brought continually before God's throne, are as incense to Him.

This is an important point to make, because you may have felt isolated in your prayers. It can be lonely, being the one watching from the boat as your loved one happily sinks beneath the current. It can be incredibly painful to bear. In future chapters, you will begin to see how God uses this suffering for His glory. For now, be encouraged that by joining other saints in your prayers for the lost, the following promise applies to you.

"… if my people who are called by my name humble themselves, and pray and seek my face and turn from their wicked ways, then I will hear from heaven and will forgive their sin and heal their land."

2 Chronicles 7:14

The Righteous Prayer

"You hypocrite, first take the log out of your own eye, and then you will see clearly to take the speck out of your brother's eye."

Matthew 7:5

We've often heard portions of this passage spoken as a retort, by non-believers and believers alike, against any sort of correction that sounds judgmental. It's been twisted. The misuse has even left a sour taste in my own mouth. When I began researching this topic of intercession, I quickly noticed a thread of commands like this one running throughout scripture.

Of course, we must make judgements (this is different than *passing judgement*). We must be able to discern whether someone is bearing fruit as a Christian. We must all hold and be held accountable in order to grow. But, before we can play teacher or spiritual leader, we must first be taught and led. This applies in prayer as well – or perhaps it applies in prayer first and foremost. Before we can pray, "fix them," we must first pray, "Lord, start with me."

This is not to say that we should stop preaching repentance. There are times when we must make someone aware of a cycle of sin they're blind to. We humans have a knack for justifying all our actions until we're convinced even God has ordained them. We all need the reality of our sins to be pointed out to us from time to time.

> *"My brothers, if anyone among you wanders from the truth and someone brings him back, let him know that whoever brings back a sinner from his wandering will save his soul from death and will cover a multitude of sins."*

> *James 5:19-20*

The metaphor of the plank does not excuse us from correction. Instead, it reminds us that when we approach the throne of God to talk about someone else's sin, we must do so humbly. We must examine ourselves first, and be sure that we're coming from a place of compassion and not smug self-righteousness.

> *"The end of all things is at hand; therefore be self-controlled and sober-minded for the sake of your prayers."*

> *1 Peter 4:7*

Being "sober-minded" is a way of saying we should not take on this task of intercession lightly. This is why it's so important to begin with our own hearts in alignment with God's Word before we worry about someone else.

We will never be completely faultless this side of heaven. The list of all the things God is working on in me could fill libraries! Thankfully, while we allow God to continue His work in us, we don't have to obtain perfection before we go to Him in prayer for the lost. Scripture provides us with a list of specific actions and attitudes that will hinder our prayers. These are a good place to begin our self-assessment.

Have I hurt someone?

> *"So if you are offering your gift at the altar and there remember that your brother has something against you, leave your gift there before the altar and go. First be reconciled to your brother, and then come and offer your gift."*
>
> *Matthew 5:23-24*

Am I harboring resentment?

> *"But if you have bitter jealousy and selfish ambition in your hearts, do not boast and be false to the truth. This is not the wisdom that comes down from above, but is earthly, unspiritual, demonic."*
>
> *James 3:14-15*

Am I demonstrating God's character to my spouse and immediate loved ones?

> *"Likewise, husbands, live with your wives in an understanding way, showing honor to the woman as the weaker vessel, since they are heirs with you of the grace of life, so that your prayers may not be hindered."*
>
> *1 Peter 3:7*

Am I using my voice to both praise God and curse His creation?

"With it we bless our Lord and Father, and with it we curse people who are made in the likeness of God."

James 3:9

If we find ourselves to be lacking in any of any of these areas, the next step is to repent and turn away from that wrongdoing. Only then can we walk forward in righteousness and continue to intercede on behalf of others, knowing that God will hear us.

"Therefore, confess your sins to one another and pray for one another, that you may be healed. The prayer of a righteous person has great power as it is working."

James 5:16

"The Lord is far from the wicked, but he hears the prayer of the righteous."

Proverbs 15:29

The Persistent Prayer

"… but afterward he said to himself, 'Though I neither fear God nor respect man, yet because this widow keeps bothering me, I will give her justice, so that she will not beat me down by her continual coming.'" And the Lord said, "Hear what the unrighteous judge says. And will not God give justice to his elect, who cry to him day and night? Will he delay long over them?'"

Luke 18:4–7

The parable of the woman and the unjust ruler is a favorite among Sunday School stories. It teaches us that if an evil man will heed the pleas of the innocent, how much more will God who is just hear us. It's a simple concept. But it is easy to become discouraged when you have prayed so diligently and haven't seen tangible results.

If you are feeling this way, then it's possible the answer is just around the corner! Be encouraged by Paul's words to the Galatian church:

> *"And let us not grow weary of doing good, for in due season we will reap, if we do not give up."*

> *Galatians 6:9*

I am a product of persistent, ceaseless prayer. I can tell you with certainty that God is moved by this type of intercession.

An early example of this is found in Genesis, in the story of Abraham and Lot. If you aren't familiar with the story, I encourage you to read Genesis 13-19. In the meantime, I will summarize it for you.

Lot was Abraham's nephew. Their families and herds of sheep dwelt together. Eventually, their herds became so large they could not be supported on the same land.

> *"Then Abram said to Lot, "Let there be no strife between you and me, and between your herdsmen and my herdsmen, for we are kinsmen. Is not the whole land before you? Separate yourself from me."*

> *Genesis 13:8-9*

Lot looked around, and saw that the land near Sodom had good resources.

> *"Abram settled in the land of Canaan, while Lot settled among the cities of the valley and moved his tent as far as Sodom."*

> *Genesis 13:12*

Fast forward a few chapters. God has made His promise to Abraham to make him the father of nations. Ishmael has been born to Hagar. Isaac has been promised to Sarah. Then, Abraham is visited by two angels of the Lord. The story of Lot picks up there.

Abraham's Prayer

"Then the Lord said, 'Because the outcry against Sodom and Gomorrah is great and their sin is very grave, I will go down to see whether they have done altogether according to the outcry that has come to me. And if not, I will know.' So the men turned from there and went toward Sodom, but Abraham still stood before the Lord. Then Abraham drew near and said, 'Will you indeed sweep away the righteous with the wicked? Suppose there are fifty righteous within the city. Will you then sweep away the place and not spare it for the fifty righteous who are in it? Far be it from you to do such a thing, to put the righteous to death with the wicked, so that the righteous fare as the wicked! Far be that from you! Shall not the Judge of all the earth do what is just?' And the Lord said, 'If I find at Sodom fifty righteous in the city, I will spare the whole place for their sake.'"

Genesis 18:20-26

As the angels of the Lord were on their way to judge Sodom and Gomorrah, Abraham remained in the presence of God begging for the cities to be spared. Reading the account of his petition, you can almost hear the agony in his voice. "Surely you will not destroy the good people along with the evil ones!" You may recognize this tone as your own while you pleaded with the Lord to spare your children, siblings, parents, or friends.

God said to Abraham that if there were fifty righteous men, he would spare the cities. But Abraham knew there weren't that many who were righteous. He kept bargaining with God.

> *"Then he said, 'Oh let not the Lord be angry, and I will speak again but this once. Suppose ten are found there.' He answered, 'For the sake of ten I will not destroy it.'"*

> *Genesis 18:32*

When the angels arrived in Sodom, Lot found them and begged them to sleep at his house because it was dangerous in the street. The men of the city came and demanded that the men of God come out so they could use them. Lot offered them his daughters instead, but the Sodomites said they would do even worse things to Lot. The angels struck the Sodomites with blindness, then they told Lot to gather all his relatives because the city would be destroyed the next day.

This paints quite a vivid picture. Lot had chosen to live in Sodom because the land was plentiful. He was blinded by its riches. And his family members weren't unaffected by the evil around them. Not only did his sons-in-law refuse to leave the cities, but his wife looked back as they were running and she was destroyed. Lot himself was ready to give his daughters up to be abused. There was no righteousness in this family. As we already know, there were not even ten righteous found there in order to spare the cities. Still, keep reading and see what God did.

> *"But he lingered. So the men seized him and his wife and his two daughters by the hand, the Lord being merciful to him, and they brought him out and set him outside the city."*

> *Genesis 19:16*

Even as they were mourning the loss of their comfortable lifestyle, God was merciful to them and the angels took them out of danger.

This is not the same mercy that was shown to Noah. Noah was spared – him and all humanity with him – because he served God. Lot and his wife and daughters were evil. God did not show mercy because Lot was righteous. He showed mercy because Abraham was righteous, and because Abraham had moved God with his persistent prayer.

Lot's Prayer

In the New Testament, we're told that as a result of God's mercy, Lot was "greatly distressed by the sensual conduct of the wicked," and "he was tormenting his soul" over the sin in his life. (*2 Peter 2:6-9*) We don't see this internal conflict in Genesis, only the outward sinful actions. Still, Peter describes Lot's contrite spirit and the faith he placed in the God of Abraham. Although Lot struggled with debauchery throughout his life (see *Genesis 19:30-38*), it grieved him, and he was called righteous.

As you begin to see God working in your loved one's heart, don't be too quick to *fix* all their issues. Remember, "man looks on the outward appearance, but the Lord looks on the heart." (*1 Samuel 16:7*)

By God's mercy, your loved one may be miraculously and instantaneously delivered from their addictions and strongholds. Be prepared, however, for your intercession efforts to double once your loved one chooses to pick up their cross. Their enemy is prowling, seeking out their weaknesses (*1 Peter 5:8*), even more so once they become a threat to his dark kingdom. They may require a lifetime of counseling, therapy, medical or psychological treatment, and abounding patience and grace. And they certainly will always need your prayers.

The Mournful Prayer

"He regards the prayer of the destitute and does not despise their prayer."

Psalm 102:17

If you are a parent, then no doubt you know the anguish of seeing your own child in pain. They look up at you with tear-filled eyes and a questioning expression. You cannot take the pain away, and you cannot explain it to them. They're learning, perhaps for the first time, that pain is a part of life for everyone, and their happy world is now changed forever.

Whether you have children or not, certainly you've faced heartache in your life. There may have been times when you've questioned what you were born to do, times when you've been rejected, attacked or betrayed. Perhaps you've even been abused, or experienced medical or mental health crises. In those times, prayers that you sent up were not in vain. God's ear is specially attuned to the cries of the broken.

"The Lord is near to the brokenhearted and saves the crushed in spirit."

Psalm 34:18

The times in my own life when I was far from God happened to coincide with the most traumatic events I've walked through. I was abused, lost pregnancies, spent a period of time couch-surfing when I couldn't afford a place to live. I turned to alcohol and questionable relationships to numb myself. My heart was raging, and I was convinced that God couldn't hear me. I banged on heaven with clinched fists, daring God to open up and face me, to explain Himself.

Even while I was fighting against Him, God heard my mother's prayers for me. Like a father witnessing his child's confusion from a hurt too big to understand, He was aching for her, and for me. I wouldn't realize this until years later. Now, I can look back and see His hand so evidently protecting me from even worse circumstances. I'll share more of my story later on.

Hannah's Prayer

"She was deeply distressed and prayed to the Lord and wept bitterly. And she vowed a vow and said, 'O Lord of hosts, if you will indeed look on the affliction of your servant and remember me and not forget your servant, but will give to your servant a son, then I will give him to the Lord all the days of his life, and no razor shall touch his head.'... And Elkanah knew Hannah his wife, and the Lord remembered her. And in due time Hannah

conceived and bore a son, and she called his name Samuel, for she said, "I have asked for him from the Lord.'"

1 Samuel 1:10-11; 19-20

This passage contains what is in my opinion one of the most beautiful phrases in scripture. *"The Lord remembered her."* This makes me think back to the bowls of incense brought continually before the throne in heaven[2]. Our prayers don't just float up and dissipate among the clouds. They're recorded permanently, and God is reminded of them continually.

The story of Hannah is close to my heart. There was a time when I thought I would never have children. A doctor told me so after my third miscarriage. I was young, and I was grieving, and I didn't ask for proof. That statement simply sealed it for me. I resigned myself to a childless existence. For years, I battled with bitterness and it was painful for me to be around children.

I can imagine being mocked by a woman who was able to give my husband children when I couldn't. I can picture myself kneeling before God, with such a weight on my chest that I couldn't force any sound from my lips. This is how Hannah prayed. And the Lord remembered her and answered. Her son would go on to be the prophet Samuel who anointed David.

We can see here a pattern emerging, that whenever God answers a prayer, it always glorifies Him in the end. When we pray in a way that inclines God's heart toward us, He will not just put a bandage on our problem – **He will use it**.

"Blessed be the God and Father of our Lord Jesus Christ, the Father of mercies and God of all comfort, who comforts us in all our affliction, so that we may be able to comfort

---

[2] Revelation 5:8

those who are in any affliction, with the comfort
with which we ourselves are comforted by God."

2 Corinthians 1:3-4

My mother wept in prayer for me for over a decade while I was estranged from God. Now that I'm a mother myself, I regret the agony she must have endured, the worry that something might happen to me before I was ready to meet Jesus. I pray so often for my children to feel God's presence, to learn to love and trust Him from a young age. I'm sometimes physically overcome with fear when I think of my children enduring any of the experiences I did, and doing so without the Lord.

That, I suppose, is the point. We were created for empathy. We're told that the purpose for our suffering is to experience God's comfort so that we can, in turn, comfort others. The desperation we feel in our souls when we see a loved one drowning in sin is what drives us to seek God on their behalf.

In Matthew 5, Jesus lists what we have nicknamed the Beatitudes. Those who possess these attributes are assigned special blessings according to their natures.

"Blessed are the poor in spirit, for theirs is the kingdom of heaven.

Blessed are those who mourn, for they shall be comforted…

Blessed are those who hunger and thirst for righteousness, for they shall be satisfied."

Matthew 5:3-4, 6

The poor in spirit are the brokenhearted. This includes those who are broken before God because of the knowledge of their sin. *The kingdom of heaven is theirs.*

Those who mourn may include you, who grieve for the lost and long for their salvation. *You will be comforted.*

Those who hunger and thirst for righteousness are the lost souls who become saved. They possess a keen awareness of how close they were to hell and the price that was paid to rescue them. They long for righteousness more than water or food. *They will be satisfied.*

The Collective Prayer

"Then Daniel went to his house and made the matter known to Hananiah, Mishael, and Azariah, his companions, and told them to seek mercy from the God of heaven concerning this mystery, so that Daniel and his companions might not be destroyed with the rest of the wise men of Babylon. Then the mystery was revealed to Daniel in a vision of the night. Then Daniel blessed the God of heaven...."

Daniel 2:17-19

Daniel was one of the bright young people who was taken to Babylon to be educated under King Nebuchadnezzar's decree. With him were Hananiah, Mishael and Azariah (better known by their Babylonian names: Shadrack, Meshack and Abednego). When Daniel found out that all the young men were going to be executed if no one could interpret the king's dream, he set a time to go before the king. Then, he went back to his friends and asked them to intercede on his behalf. When the answer inevitably came through, he gave all the glory to God.

Another, perhaps even more famous, example of collective prayer comes from Matthew.

> *"Then Jesus went with them to a place called Gethsemane, and he said to his disciples, 'Sit here, while I go over there and pray.' And taking with him Peter and the two sons of Zebedee, he began to be sorrowful and troubled. Then he said to them, 'My soul is very sorrowful, even to death; remain here, and watch with me.'"*

> *Matthew 26:36-38*

Even Jesus, who is the ultimate example for us to imitate, found himself in need of support via prayer. As we will discuss in more detail in future chapters, Jesus specifically instructed his disciples to pray together. This type of collective intercession is so powerful, Jesus tells us that when even a few are gathered and agreeing together in prayer, He is there with them.

> *"Again I say to you, if two of you agree on earth about anything they ask, it will be done for them by my Father in heaven. For where two or three are gathered in my name, there am I among them."*

> *Matthew 18:19-20*

We're promised that the collective prayer of the church heals the sick and has the power to bring about the forgiveness of a person's sins.

> *"Is anyone among you sick? Let him call for the elders of the church... And the prayer of faith will save the one who is sick, and the Lord will raise him up. And if he has committed sins, he will be forgiven."*

> *James 5:14-15*

21

If you have been fervently praying for a loved one to find Jesus, and you have felt isolated and powerless in those prayers, then perhaps you need to reach out to the church. This doesn't have to be a church building or organization. Remember His promise – it only takes a few. Open up to someone who you know to be sincere in their faith. Ask them to remember your loved one in prayer whenever they go before God. Set up a weekly or monthly time to get together and lift your voices to God in unison.

> *"Two are better than one, because they have a good reward for their toil."*
>
> *Ecclesiastes 4:9*
>
> *"And let us consider how to stir up one another to love and good works, not neglecting to meet together, as is the habit of some, but encouraging one another, and all the more as you see the Day drawing near."*
>
> *Hebrews 10:24-25*

Another thing to consider along the lines of this topic is the fellowship of the church. With sermons being so readily available to watch online, it can be tempting to avoid physically attending a church service. At least, it is for me. Any type of social gathering at which face-to-face interaction is guaranteed is terrifying for me. I have learned to override those stress signals and push through, but I will need to spend the rest of the day – and sometimes the next day – recuperating. I have often used this as an excuse not to attend church in person.

When Covid-19 reached the states and everything shut down, I used fear as an excuse not to attend. When everything finally started back up, my kids were going through a phase of being difficult to corral. So, I used my kids as an excuse not to attend. I am thankful that God did not give up on me once I was saved and called. He continues to push me out of my comfort zones into scary places so I can grow.

My husband and I started bringing our kids to church only recently. We found that every Saturday night or Sunday morning, there was some reason that we could easily use to stay home. The kids didn't sleep well, someone had a tummy ache, the shirt I wanted to wear was dirty. Once, my husband and I had a small argument and we each stated we didn't feel like being in church with that on our minds.

My mother counseled me wisely, telling me that the days we don't feel like going to church are probably the days we need it the most. It only took a couple weeks for us to realize the truth of this ourselves. Each time we decided to go, we left there with our burdens lifted and our spirits filled. We learned something we didn't already know. Our children experienced the love of Jesus from others, and our daughter participated in worship. The afternoons that followed at home were peaceful. We saw that when we were obedient, the Father responded with good things.

Scripture is full of examples of God's people leaning on each other. Adam had Eve. Moses had Aaron. Daniel had Hananiah, Mishael and Azariah. Even Jesus had Peter, James and John.

This lesson may not pertain to you at this time. If you are attending church regularly, and have a steady group of prayer partners, then I am thankful and I hope you remain faithful in that regard. This lesson is one I continually refer to myself, so I ask you to pray for your brothers and sisters who struggle with this aspect of Christian life. Perhaps you can be the one to draw us in and encourage us in fellowship.

The Prayer of Faith

"And I am sure of this, that he who began a good work in you will bring it to completion at the day of Jesus Christ."

Philippians 1:6

I used to say that I had faith that God could answer me, but I had no hope that He cared to. I have an entire journal entry dedicated to that sentiment. I've come to learn that true faith encompasses the two. We have to believe that God is able, and that He is willing.

In previous chapters, we've seen evidence of God's just and merciful character. We've witnessed through scripture how inclined He is to hear us and to act. He hears the prayers of the broken, of the collective church, of the persistent intercessor.

We cannot neglect to study the single greatest aspect of prayer, the substance that gives any type of prayer its power. Faith.

"But let him ask in faith, with no doubting, for the one who doubts is like a wave of the sea that is driven and tossed by the wind. For that

person must not suppose that he will receive anything from the Lord..."

James 1:6-7

"Now faith is the assurance of things hoped for, the conviction of things not seen."

Hebrews 11:1

I recommend the whole chapter of Hebrews 11 for your personal reading. I've heard it nicknamed "the Faith Chapter." It defines faith for us as the confidence that what we have hoped for – prayed for – will come about, even though we cannot see a way. Then, after listing the evidence of God's power and mercy through examples of men like Noah and Abraham, the scripture goes on to say:

"These all died in faith, not having received the things promised, but having seen them and greeted them from afar..."

Hebrews 11:13

When we enter God's presence with the intention of interceding for the lost, we need to approach with confidence that He will send the answer even if we never see it.

My maternal grandmother is an example of this to me. Whenever I visited, I used to hear her praying for all her children and grandchildren when she thought no one else was in the house. She would walk down the hallway, touch our photos, and weep as she cried out to God. She passed away before I was saved, but I know that she went to heaven believing that He would someday answer her prayers for us.

The Sinner's Prayer

"Not everyone who says to me, 'Lord, Lord,' will enter the kingdom of heaven, but the one who does the will of my Father who is in heaven."

Matthew 7:21

Since I was a child, I professed the name of Jesus. I believed in Him wholeheartedly. Belief wasn't enough. Scripture says that even the devil believes in Jesus (*James 2:19*). As long as I was arrogant, and inwardly thinking that I could be absolved by good works or justified by the evils done to me, I couldn't obtain salvation. I prayed and cried out and God was always just a hairsbreadth out of my reach.

> *"But understand this, that in the last days there will come times of difficulty. For people will be lovers of self, lovers of money, proud, arrogant, abusive, disobedient to their parents, ungrateful, unholy, heartless, unappeasable, slanderous, without self-control, brutal, not loving good,*

> *treacherous, reckless, swollen with conceit,*
> *lovers of pleasure rather than lovers of God,*
> *having the appearance of godliness, but denying*
> *its power. Avoid such people."*

2 Timothy 3:1-5

In my youth, I generally had the appearance of godliness. I attended church several times a week, sung in choir, memorized verses, invited friends to church, gave money to the homeless, prayed as fervently as anyone in my pew. Within, I checked many of the boxes listed in 2 Timothy – I was selfish, proud, arrogant, disobedient, ungrateful, heartless, lacked self-control, and was swollen with conceit. Oh, that phrase is so hard to type. I don't think there is a more graphic depiction of a person concealing a heart full of sin than swollen with conceit.

I was married very young to an older man who became abusive very quickly. Even then, I continued trying under my own power to be good. I thought if I was just good enough then God would rescue me. I thought God would change him and I could be happy. When I left the situation for my own safety, I was turned away by friends in the church. I was called rebellious, disobedient. I had suffered three miscarriages under the abuse, and was so depressed that I was near the point of giving up on my life. I had done everything God ever asked of me – I thought – and He had abandoned me. His children had abandoned me.

I decided that if being good didn't get me anywhere, I didn't need it. I turned the opposite way down a path of self-destruction. I purposely walked into situations that felt dangerous, secretly hoping that it would end in my death. And through all this, I felt justified. I cycled through feelings of remorse, followed by intense rage and self-hatred that would morph into pleas for rescue. I couldn't understand why God never seemed to show up.

My lifestyle finally balanced enough for me to get a good job and my own apartment. During that time, I started dating Ken, the man who would later become my husband and the father of my children.

After Ken joined the army, we got married and we moved. Our relationship at that time was strained by communication breakdown and my own past trauma. I punished him for my ex-husband's actions. He was angry with me seemingly all the time. While I was pregnant with our first child, we separated for a brief period. When she was born, our collective love for her bound us together again.

Unexpectedly, I fell into a deep depression in the postpartum period. I waited over 16 months to finally ask for medication, and by then I had done so much damage in our marriage, my relationship with my daughter, and other family connections. Even with the medication and therapy, I was still trying to deal with the trauma of the past decade under my own strength. I had completely given up on seeking God. I had a brief psychotic episode in which I thought I was gay and tried to convince everyone of that, including my husband. We talked about separating again, but didn't go through with it that time. A month later, I became pregnant with our second child.

We moved across the country for Ken to start a new job. We were still fighting. We were still angry with each other and talking about divorce. We would be fine and happy one day, and completely sick of each other the next. It was an emotionally painful and confusing time, although we were enjoying the most financial freedom of our marriage thus far. It seemed that we were slowly getting on track and things were eventually going to be okay. Then, a couple of months before my son was due, something incredible happened to me.

If you've read my blog, you know this part of the story. God called me out of darkness, by showing me all my sins and letting me feel the guilt and ownership of them for the first time. All the excuses and justifications were gone. I had no one to bear the weight of them but myself, and they were so heavy. I sunk to my knees, weeping. I couldn't even vocalize my repentance. I was so broken and ashamed, but I was not shamed. God, in His mercy, showed me how He had saved me from the natural consequences of my sin. For reasons that are His own, God had kept His hand on me throughout my arrogant, rebellious years, and had chosen a time when I felt my life to be going alright to finally rescue me. Over the following few weeks, I would have more experiences like this one, when I would remember heinous sins and stop everything and repent. Each time, the burden was lifted and replaced with God's peace. By the time my son was born, praise and thanksgiving were continually on my lips (Psalm 34:1). I went into the delivery room literally singing songs of praise between contractions.

> *"If we confess our sins, He is faithful and just to forgive us our sins and to cleanse us from all unrighteousness."*

> *1 John 1:9*

> *"He himself bore our sins in his body on the tree, that we might die to sin and live to righteousness. By his wounds you have been healed."*

> *1 Peter 2:24*

In Genesis, when God called Adam and he didn't come because he was naked, God asked, who told you that you were naked? Did you eat of the tree I told you not to? Whenever I read that passage, I read it in the same tone I use when my daughter makes a mess after disregarding my advice. Why are you covered in marker? You wrote on yourself like I said not to, didn't you?

It's the kind of groan in a parent's voice that says, "I'm going to have to clean that up later."

The moment man introduced sin into the world, that sin came with a cost. A payment would be required. The moment God asked how Adam knew he was naked, was the moment God saw himself tortured, and bleeding on the cross. Our merciful, loving father, who had such a beautiful plan for this world, saw the mess we made and knew that He would be the one to clean it up. He was the only one qualified to the pay the price.

He had considered starting over completely. Humanity would reach a point where the thoughts of man's heart would be only evil continually, and it would grieve God's heart so much He would regret creation. (*Genesis 6:5-8*) But, for the sake of one righteous man, God allowed humans to continue, knowing full well it would mean Himself becoming flesh and dying in the most brutal way.

> *"So if the Son sets you free, you will be free indeed."*
>
> *John 8:36*

Once I realized how desperately I needed God's forgiveness and mercy, it inspired me to turn away from evil. Once my eyes were opened to see my sin the way God did, I was delivered from the lies of homosexuality, the blame I placed on others and the desire to sin any more. My carnal desires were replaced with a desperate longing to give glory to the God who saved me.

Scripture says that heaven rejoices when a sinner repents. (*Luke 15:10*) They become a new creation. (*2 Corinthians 5:17*) That is the power of this type of prayer. This is the prayer that your loved one will offer up when the Holy Spirit breaks their heart in answer to your fervent intercession. This is the payoff for your spiritual labor. This cannot be replaced or replicated in a series of magical words, and words may even get in the way.

When God Is Quiet

The original title of this chapter was *When God Says No*, but I changed it because I don't believe God ever refuses a prayer to save someone's soul. That's why He sent His only son to be brutally beaten and killed, and that's what most of His word talks about – salvation. I do, however, know that God is often quiet. The answer rarely comes at a time when we hope or expect it to. I also know that unfortunately, many will be lost. God will never cease to answer prayers for the lost by reaching for them, but the lost have to decide to be rescued. He won't force anyone to love Him.

> *"And then many will fall away and betray one another and hate one another. And many false prophets will arise and lead many astray. And because lawlessness will be increased, the love of many will grow cold."*
>
> *Matthew 24:10-12*

I struggled with writing this chapter, because at first glance the message doesn't seem very positive. However, I feel it necessary to tell you the truth, which is very simply that the loved one you are praying for might never come to accept Jesus.

So many books on prayer focus on a formula, on getting a result that you want. If your loved one is never saved, you could lose faith and say that all your effort was a waste. You could think that God didn't answer or prayer doesn't work. I'm here to tell you that prayer always works. God always hears and responds. It then falls to the individual to answer God's call or not.

> *"And He said, "Abba, Father, all things are possible for You. Take this cup away from Me; nevertheless, not what I will, but what You will."*

> *Mark 14:36*

Even Jesus faced this quandary. He knew the physical agony and public torment he was about to walk through, and he was terrified. He prayed so fervently to be spared from it, that he sweat blood. Even with his direct line to heaven, God had to be silent. It was the only way to save us.

> *"And this is the confidence that we have toward him, that if we ask anything according to his will he hears us."*

> *1 John 5:14*

Jesus submitted to God's will and fulfilled His mission. This is key. Whenever we pray, we must always let go of our own designs and surrender to God's. We can have an idea what this looks like by looking at scripture. From 2 Peter 3:9, we can be sure that it is His will for all to be saved.

> *"The Lord is not slow to fulfill his promise… not wishing that any should perish, but that all should reach repentance."*

While our prayers may be aligned with God's ultimate will for our loved ones, we may sometimes try to control the timeline and method for this to come about. We may pray, "Lord, please save my sister before she goes in for this major surgery." It's okay to pray this way, but we also need to understand that His timing may be different than ours. Your sister may need to walk through that trial before her heart will be opened to Him.

The bottom line is, we don't know anything, and God knows everything. When we pray for His will to be done, and we allow His peace to replace our anxiety, the answer always comes. And it's always good.

> *"And the peace of God, which surpasses all understanding, will guard your hearts and your minds in Christ Jesus."*
>
> *Philippians 4:7*

The Scriptural Prayer

"… do not be anxious about anything, but in everything by prayer and supplication with thanksgiving let your requests be made known to God. And the peace of God, which surpasses all understanding, will guard your hearts and your minds in Christ Jesus."

Philippians 4:6-7

This verse is written above my calendar and I refer to it often. A regular part of being an autistic mother constantly surrounded by stressors is frequent spikes in anxiety. I am learning to give each situation to God in prayer, and this passage is a beautifully constructed template for how to do that. Let's break it down.

Rather than being anxious, we're directed to:

• Pray

• Be thankful

• Present our requests to God

In place of the anxiety we offer up, we are instructed to:

• Accept His peace, which transcends our understanding and guards our hearts and minds in Jesus

Jesus used a similar template when he was teaching his disciples to pray. You will know this as the Lord's Prayer. It's a common prayer frequently recited on its own, but in light of the passage above we can see a pattern emerging. With the help of these two passages, we can learn to apply these basic principles to our own petitions.

Let's take a look at Matthew 6:9-13.

> *"Pray then like this: 'Our Father in heaven, hallowed be your name. Your kingdom come, your will be done, on earth as it is in heaven. Give us this day our daily bread, and forgive us our debts, as we also have forgiven our debtors. And lead us not into temptation, but deliver us from evil.'"*

Now, divided by verse, here are Jesus' instructions:

9. Praise the name of God
10. Pray for God's will
11. Pray for provision
12. Pray for forgiveness, after first forgiving others
13. Pray for help amid temptation and deliverance from evil

You may be wondering why, after all the times I stated in this book that there are no magic prayers, I am now outlining a template for prayer. Please, when you apply these principles, do not simply regurgitate the words and phrases. That is not at all the point I'm making here.

I know from experience that it is easy to become distracted during prayer time. Our thoughts can drift to other things, causing us to mentally wander from God's presence. But our prayers are only as effective as our communion with God and alignment with His will.

When we apply the instructions Jesus left for his disciples, we can stay focused on the reason for our entering God's presence in the first place. The fact that we can come to Him freely shouldn't mean that we come to Him flippantly.

> *"Be not rash with your mouth, nor let your heart be hasty to utter a word before God, for God is in heaven and you are on earth. Therefore let your words be few."*
>
> *Ecclesiastes 5:2*

Let's not forget who we are talking to when we pray. This is the God who spoke and the seas separated from the sky. He breathed into dust and Adam lived. He has the power to end the world with a thought, and we have earned that, yet He has chosen again and again to love us. When we present our requests before His throne, let's show Him the reverence He is due.

Here is a basic example of how I apply these concepts in my own daily prayers.

God, I praise you for being holy. Thank you for saving me and sustaining me. Please have your will in my life, and guide the steps of my husband according to your will. Please continue to provide for us as you always have. Thank you for my husband's job. Please continue to guide his decisions and give him favor so we can support our children. Please forgive me for falling short, and please help me to be a better mother, wife and friend. Please protect my children and help them to know you from a young age. Please chase after my loved one who is lost and running from you. Please don't give up on them. Give them at least one more chance to turn to you, and call out to them in a way they cannot deny. I ask these things in the name of Jesus. I know you have heard and will answer.

When we go to God to petition Him for a lost soul, we should not neglect the other aspects of prayer. We should always praise Him, we should always ask forgiveness, and we should always pray for His will to be done. This is how we will remain surrendered to Him and aware of the peace He answers with.

Final Thoughts

"And this gospel of the kingdom will be proclaimed throughout the whole world as a testimony to all nations, and then the end will come."

Matthew 24:14

We have been living in the end times for centuries. The signs are everywhere that we are running out of time. While we cannot lose our sense of urgency in our evangelism, we also need to practice trust that God means what He says. He promised that the end will not come until everyone has had a fair chance to choose Him. That means that, along with bearing witness to His glory when opportunities arise, we need to be vigilant in our prayers. Knowing that only the Holy Spirit can convict and draw a person's soul, our prayers – more than our words – carry significant weight in these final days before the end.

If I can make one final suggestion, it would be to keep track of your prayers so that you can look back and see how God has answered them over time. This isn't necessarily a biblical idea, but it's something that has encouraged me. Write your prayers down on a napkin, a church bulletin, keep it in your Bible or write them in the back of this book. Record them somehow, and then refer to them at a later day and time. Then, watch God work.

> *"Now to him who is able to do far more abundantly than all that we ask or think, according to the power at work within us, to him be glory in the church and in Christ Jesus throughout all generations, forever and ever. Amen."*
>
> *Ephesians 3:20-21*

Prayer Journal

CADIENTE

_____ / _____ / _____

_____
_____
_____
_____
_____
_____
_____
_____
_____
_____
_____
_____
_____
_____
_____
_____
_____
_____
_____
_____
_____
_____
_____
_____
_____
_____
_____

PRAYER THAT SAVES

_____ / _____ / _____

_____
_____
_____
_____
_____
_____
_____
_____
_____
_____
_____
_____
_____
_____
_____
_____
_____
_____
_____
_____
_____
_____
_____
_____
_____
_____
_____

CADIENTE

_____ / _____ / _____

_____
_____
_____
_____
_____
_____
_____
_____
_____
_____
_____
_____
_____
_____
_____
_____
_____
_____
_____
_____
_____
_____
_____
_____
_____
_____
_____

PRAYER THAT SAVES

_____ / _____ / _____

CADIENTE

_____/ _____/ _____

_____/_____/_____

_____

_____

_____

_____

_____

_____

_____

_____

_____

_____

_____

_____

_____

_____

_____

_____

_____

_____

_____

_____

_____

_____

_____

_____

_____

_____

_____

CADIENTE

_____/ _____/ _____

Acknowledgements

My deepest appreciation to my parents, Ron and Analita Ray, for joining their hands and hearts with me on this project. Their contributions as editors, spiritual advisors, and prayer partners are invaluable.

My love and gratitude to my patient husband, Ken, for taking other responsibilities off my shoulders so I could devote time to the completion of this book.

My love and thanks to my sweet children, Ember and Jack, for their inspiring innocence and unconditional admiration.

www.ingramcontent.com/pod-product-compliance
Lightning Source LLC
Chambersburg PA
CBHW071935020426
42331CB00010B/2888